£3·99

DIVINE LOVE

SELWYN HUGHES

Illustrated by Brian Norwood

© CWR 1990

CWR, Waverley Abbey House,
Waverley Lane, Farnham, Surrey GU9 8EP

NATIONAL DISTRIBUTORS
Australia: Christian Marketing Pty Ltd., PO Box 154, North Geelong, Victoria 3215   Tel: (052) 786100
Canada: Canadian Christian Distributors Inc., PO Box 550, Virgil, Ontario LOS 1TO   Tel: 416 641 0631
Republic of Ireland: Merrion Press Ltd, 10 D'Olier Street, Dublin Tel & Fax 773316
Malaysia: Salvation Book Centre, (M) Sdn. Bhd., 23 Jalan SS2/64, 47300 Petaling Jaya, Selangor
New Zealand: CWR (NZ), PO Box 4108, Mount Maunganui 3030 Tel: (075) 757412
Singapore: Alby Commercial Enterprises Pte Ltd., Garden Hotel, 14 Balmoral Road, Singapore 1025
Southern Africa: CWR (Southern Africa), PO Box 43 Kenilworth, 7745, RSA Tel: (021) 7612560

Typeset by Watermark, Cromer

Printed in Great Britain by
BPCC Paulton Books Limited

ISBN 1–85345–038–3 Hardback
ISBN 1–85345–039–1 Limp
First published 1985 and reprinted in illustrated format 1990

Unless otherwise stated, all Scripture quotations are from the Holy Bible, New International Version. Copyright © 1973, 1978, 1984, International Bible Society

INTRODUCTION

The world is crying out for love. Popular songs, for example, further that cry: "What the world needs now is love sweet love" and "All you need is love". They may be calling for a greater evidence of love but they all miss the ultimate expression of love, *the divine love* that is only found in one source: God.

In many ways, the Christian church can also miss out on that expression of divine love. Each Christian carries within themselves their own unique and very limited concept of God, often influenced and distorted by negative experiences in their developmental years.

1 John 4: 8 tells us: 'God is *love*'. It doesn't say God is loving, or God is lovely, or that God has love.

Our very language restricts our understanding of this powerful truth – 'God is love'. The Welsh language gets nearest to the heart of 1 John 4: 8 by declaring 'God love *is*'. To put it another way, the reason for God's existence is love. He does not love to exist: He exists to love.

My prayer is that as you meditate on the divine love of God your lives will be enriched to the point where you know deep in your heart that 'God is *love*'.

Selwyn Hughes

LOVE — THE HIGHEST VALUE

Professor Henry Drummond once preached a spectacular sermon on 1 Corinthians 13, under the title "The Greatest Thing in the World." At the heart of this deeply moving sermon was this statement: "We have become accustomed to being told that the greatest thing in the world is faith. Well, we are wrong. Paul lists three great qualities in 1 Corinthians 13 and stands them up together — faith, hope and love. But which is the greatest? Without a moment's hesitation the decision falls — 'the greatest of these is love'."

Faith hope love
love greatest

1 Corinthians 13

This is a gripping and exciting theme. First we underline the supremacy of love — then we shall examine some of its qualities and characteristics. We begin by pondering the circumstances which surround Christ's words in Mark 12:30–31. What an important moment it was in the history of the universe when that lawyer stood up and asked Jesus the question: "Of all the commandments, which is the most important?"

Love god +
neighbour

Mark 12:28–34

According to Josephus, a Jewish historian, Israel had at that time more than 3,600 commandments: which one of these would Jesus choose? If he chose the wrong one, then His followers would go wrong with Him — but if He chose the right one, then his followers would go right with Him. The ages held their breath, for it was a critical moment. The future hung in the balance. Christ went unerringly to the highest: "You must love the Lord your God with your whole heart, with your whole soul, with your whole mind, and with your whole strength . . . You must love your neighbour as yourself" (Moffatt). Nothing higher can be imagined or conceived. It is the ultimate in values.

vv. 30–31

We must ask ourselves: was this emphasis unique to Jesus? Did the founder of Christianity stress something only for it to be softened by His followers? Not so. Admittedly, it appears at times that Paul, His chief interpreter, makes *faith* the supreme value, but when he is obliged to make a definite choice, he says: "And now these three remain: faith, hope and love. But the greatest of these is love" (1 Cor. 13:13, NIV). As one writer puts it: "Paul takes the torch from his Master's hand and holds up love as the highest and supreme value."

1 Corinthians 13:13

A casual examination of John's letters might give the impression that he, too, appears to give the highest value to something other than love. He speaks a great deal about 'knowledge', and in fact uses the word 'know' 36 times. Does this mean that John believes 'knowledge' to be the highest value? No. When it

comes to the *supreme* emphasis, he places that on 'love' and uses the word 43 times. John, writing against a background of Gnosticism — the so-called 'knowers' — was bound to mention the word 'know' a number of times, but there can be little doubt that his *supreme* emphasis lay where Jesus and Paul put it — on love.

Peter also takes the torch from his Master's hand when he, too, makes love the supreme value: "Add to your faith goodness . . . knowledge . . . self-control . . . perseverance . . . godliness . . . brotherly kindness . . . *love*" (2 Pet. 1:5–7, NIV). So the three greatest interpreters of the Gospel all make love the supreme value. And for all those who follow Christ, it cannot be otherwise.

2 Peter 1:5–7

1 Peter 4:1–11

v. 8

Scripture everywhere affirms love as supreme, but

what is the verdict of those who do not believe Scripture to be infallible and do not accept it as their guide?

The surprising thing is that the scientists and psychologists of our age are increasingly agreeing that 'love' is the most constructive element in the universe. Dr Carl Menninger, one of the foremost names in the field of modern-day psychiatry, wrote a book entitled, *Love Against Hate*. He took the position that the main reason why people break down is because they have not been loved and have not learned to love. This understanding proved to be a turning-point in psychiatry, for prior to this, many people had accepted the idea that insight is the cure-all for personality problems. "Give the person insight as to his troubles", it was said, "and he will be cured."

Insight, however, is not necessarily curative. I know

many people who have great insight into their problems, but lack the motivation to do anything about them. Menninger stumbled upon a principle of the universe — that love builds up and hate tears down — and many others are also coming to that conclusion. Is scientific investigation, then, leading to the same conclusion as revelation — that love is the supreme value in human nature? Inevitably so.

It stands to reason that if the greatest thing about God is the fact that He is perfect love, then the universe which He created is also designed to run on love. If science is, as someone described it, "thinking God's thoughts after Him", then, sooner or later, open-minded scientists must admit that God has written into the universe, not only His power, but His character also. And what is His character? 1 John 4:8 tells us: "God is *love*."

1 John 4:1–12

1 John 4:8

Notice carefully what the text is saying. It is not just telling us that God is loving. Neither is it just saying that God is lovely. It is not even saying that God *has* love. It is saying much more than this. The Welsh version puts it in this way: "God love *is*." In other words, the reason for God's existence is love. He does not love to exist: He exists to love. I have used the following illustration many times before to explain the text "God is love", as it helps to clarify what John is really saying. If you take love out of an angel, what do you have left? A devil. If you take love out of a human being, what do you have left? A sinner. If you take love out of God — what do you have left? Nothing — for God *is* love. Love is not something God does: love is what He is.

We have seen that Dr Carl Menninger came to the conclusion that people experience deep psychological conflicts because they have not loved or been loved.

When Dr Menninger gained this new insight, he called his staff together and explained that the new diagnosis demanded new treatment. He said, in essence: "These people are in our psychiatric wards because they haven't loved or been loved. *So we will have to love them into loving.* We will have to make all our contacts with our patients love contacts, from the top psychiatrist to the caretakers. If you go to change an electric light bulb in a patient's room, you must make your contact a love contact." They tried it for six months and found that, at the end of this period, the length of time which their patients had to spend in hospital was cut in half. The patients were getting well in half the time it took under the old 'give them insight' technique. Love was the key.

Romans
13:7–14

Another psychiatrist, Dr Smiley Blanton, came to a similar conclusion in his book, *Love or Perish*, when he said: "If you don't love, you perish — not in hell necessarily, but now as a personality. Nothing will hold the personality together except love. So love — or perish." Personally, I find it quite fascinating how some of the world's foremost social scientists are beginning to discover in their various fields the truth of what the Bible has been saying for generations — namely, that love is the highest value in the universe. Of course, they are a long way yet from seeing that the highest expression of love is love for God — but that is not discovered by scientific experimentation. Only the Holy Spirit can show them that.

When Dr John Plokker, head of a large mental hospital in Holland, was asked what was the deepest necessity in human nature, he replied: "To love and be loved." He said that in his hospital, they had to put on extra nurses to have what they called 'loving hours' — hours when they could give babies, not merely service, but love.

You may have heard of the famous experiment which took place many years ago at Bellevue Hospital, New York, when it was discovered that orphaned babies, though given scientific care and feeding, died of minor ailments at the rate of 32 per cent during the first year of life. They looked carefully into the problem and came to the conclusion that the babies were getting everything except love. They recruited 'love volunteers' — suitable women who would come in to the hospital and love the babies for a few hours each day. The superintendent reported, "We could no more do without these 'love volunteers' than we could do without penicillin."

One of the members of a church of which I was once pastor had been bedridden for many years. She spoke very little to people who visited her and was deeply withdrawn. A Christian nurse said to me, "What she needs is love" — and set out to give it to her. In her spare time she ministered to this woman in the most loving way I have ever seen. In a few days, the woman opened up and began to talk. After a month, she was out of bed and well. Love had set her free.

If love, working on a horizontal level, carries such transforming power, then what of the love that exists on a vertical level — the love of God for men and the love of men for God? Such divine love has power beyond all telling.

Philippians
1:1–11
v. 9

LOVE — ALL EMBRACING

Love is not only primary; it embraces the whole person. Never was love defined as being so embracing and so deep as in Jesus' immortal words: "Love the Lord your God with all your heart, and with all your soul, and with all your mind, and with all your strength" (Mark 12:30). The call is to love God totally.

Deuteronomy
6:1–13
v. 5
Mark 12:30

The mature and balanced person is the one who loves the Lord his God with every part of his being — the whole person wholly devoted to God. Some love God with all the strength of the mind, but are weak in other areas of their being. These are the intellectuals in Christianity — brilliant, but not very lovable. Some love God with all the strength of the soul — the affectional part of our being — but never cultivate the same degree of strength in other areas. These are the sentimentalists in Christianity — a lot of heat, but not much light.

Both types of Christians are immature. The only mature person is the one who loves the Lord his God with the strength of the heart, the strength of the soul, the strength of the mind and the strength of the body — the whole person devoted to God. If you think this is a high standard, then remember that the God who *demands* total love is the God who *gives* you His total love.

It's interesting to note that the words, "with all your mind", are not included in the original commandment which God gave to Israel in Deuteronomy 6:4. Why did Jesus insert these additional words? No one can really say for sure — we can only speculate. For myself, I am grateful that Jesus added that extra phrase, for by so

Deuteronomy
6:4

doing He has underlined for all time the importance of love being the controlling force of the mind.

Some years ago, when the atomic power station was built at Oak Ridge in the USA, a report stated that more people went to church in that area than in any other part of America. An observer asked the question: "Are these people more frightened?" The answer was given, "No, not frightened — *reverent*. They are in the presence of a great mystery — and it drives them to their knees." These people recognised that love must control the energy which modern minds have discovered, or else we shall perish — literally perish.

One of the scientists who manned the atomic station at Oak Ridge became a minister of the Gospel, and when questioned about this by the Press, gave the following reply: "I have come to see the necessity of the Christian faith, with its emphasis on love, as the controlling force in this age of atomic energy." The words, "You shall love the Lord your God with all your *mind*", are an up-to-the minute imperative.

Philippians 2.1–11

v. 5

This absolute commandment expressed in this absolute form is as necessary to existence in this universe as the law of gravity. For, with it, life holds together; without it, life falls apart. One commentator believes that the whole of human history, as well as the history of individual lives, is a commentary on the fact that if we don't love God totally, then we can't love ourselves in a healthy and balanced way. A divided self is a despised self. What it amounts to is this: if we don't live with God in the harmony of love, then we will have to live with ourselves in the disharmony of hate.

1 John 4:16–21

At this point I must pick up once again the words of

Jesus in Mark chapter 12, where He responded to an Mark 12:31 enquirer's request as to what was the greatest commandment. You may have noticed that in answer to this request, Jesus also gave a second commandment which we have not yet considered: "Love your neighbour as yourself" (v. 31, NIV). If Jesus had stopped at the first and had not gone on to give the second, then humanity would have been clear about its relationship with God, but not so clear about its relationship with man. Love for God must be manifested in love to man. And Jesus added: "There is no commandment greater than these."

This means that the issue is no longer open to debate. To question it, is as pointless as questioning the statement, "Two and two makes four." We must take it or leave it — with results or consequences.

LOVE — YOUR NEIGHBOUR AND YOURSELF

We must now examine in detail that second commandment, "Love your neighbour as yourself", and we begin by asking ourselves: who is our 'neighbour'? In Leviticus 19:18, a 'neighbour' is defined in this way: "Do not seek revenge or bear a grudge against one of your people, but love your neighbour as yourself". It is clear, then, that the Old Testament definition of a 'neighbour' meant a person of one's own race or religion.

Leviticus 19:18

In Luke 10:29 a lawyer who "wanted to justify himself" asked Jesus: "And who is my neighbour?" This question prompted Jesus to relate the story of the Good Samaritan, in which He defined a neighbour as someone of another race who is in need. There can be little doubt that in Jesus' mind, the term 'neighbour' means anyone, anywhere, who is in need. It's interesting to note that the hero in Jesus' story is not a Jew playing the bountiful brother to a helpless member of another race, but a despised Samaritan ministering to a Jew. In the deft strokes of this story, Jesus demolishes any pride or arrogance that may have been in the hearts of His Jewish listeners, and broadens the Old Testament definition of the word 'neighbour' to mean not just a member of one's own race or religion, but any person, anywhere.

Luke 10:25–37 v. 29

The love we are to have toward our 'neighbour' is not to be more or less than our love for ourselves, but *as*. This is terribly important. It balances self-love and other-love in exact proportion.

Galatians 5:13–25 v. 14

Those who study human behaviour tell us that there are three powerful urges in our human nature — self,

sex and the herd or social urge. The self urge is obviously self-regarding. The herd urge is obviously other-regarding. The sex urge is partly self-regarding and partly other-regarding.

If we accept these categories for the moment, then it means that there are two driving urges within us — self-regarding, and other-regarding. Some call them the egoistic and altruistic urges. Some organise their lives around the self-regarding urge, and become egocentric in their attitudes and actions. Such people are unhappy because they are at conflict within themselves. And why? Because the other-regarding urge is not expressed. A self-centred person is an unhappy person — in conflict with himself.

Others organise their lives around the other-regarding urge, and become herd-centred people.

They, too, are at war with themselves, for the self-regarding urge is unexpressed — hence frustrated. Life organised around the self is individualism. Life organised around the herd is collectivism. Both are unbalanced positions and inevitably produce unfulfilled and unsatisfied people. Jesus steps into this conflict and offers something that meets the needs of self and the herd: "Love your neighbour (the other-regarding urge) as yourself (the self-regarding urge)." Both are balanced exactly.

In James 2:8, James calls this principle of 'loving your neighbour as yourself' the *royal law*. Why the 'royal' law? One commentator says: "Because you belong to royalty (i.e. heaven's royalty) if you obey that law." Some Christians are greatly perplexed about this whole idea of 'loving' ourselves. They say: "Are we not

James
2:1–13
v. 8

taught in Scripture to crucify the self and put it to death on the Cross? Isn't 'love of self' an obnoxious weed to be uprooted from the human heart?"

In order to understand the thought we are discussing here, we must differentiate between self-love and love of self. Love of self is an obnoxious thing — narcissism. But self-love is the healthy regard one has for oneself and is, in my judgment, a necessary part of maturity.

A personal illustration might help to bring the matter more clearly into focus. I was brought up in a Christian environment where I was taught that the 'self' is an obnoxious thing and must be daily nailed to the Cross. The most popular hymn in our church was one in which the last lines of each verse went thus: "All of self, and none of Thee"; "Some of self, and some of Thee"; "None of self, and all of Thee".

There is nothing wrong with that hymn, of course, but the impression I got both from the preaching and the choice of hymns was that the 'self' must be eliminated. It was well-intentioned but seriously misleading. We cannot eliminate the self, sex and herd instincts, for they are an integral part of us, and without them we would be ciphers — nobodies.

I learned later, through studying the Scriptures for myself, that while there were things in me of which I could not approve, those things were not a barrier to me accepting myself. Acceptance must not be seen as being the same as approval, of course. I cannot approve of the things in me which are unlike Christ, but I can nevertheless accept myself and allow the Holy Spirit to bring about those changes within me which He desires to achieve. I can now love the type of

Romans
8:1–17
v. 16

person I am — love myself in spite of the marginal faults and blemishes — for the central 'me' is loveable: he is consenting to redemption. And the real secret, of course, of being able to love myself in a healthy and positive way is that I love Someone more than myself. I love myself in God.

LOVE — WHAT IS IT?

Having seen something of love's primacy and its scope, we must now focus on its *nature*. We ask ourselves, therefore: what is the meaning of love? How do we define it? What are its ingredients and what is its true essence?

Ashley Montagu, in his book *The Meaning of Love*, gives a dictionary definition which reads thus: "Love is a feeling of deep regard, fondness, devotion; deep affection, usually accompanied by a yearning or a desire for; affection between persons of opposite sex, more or less founded on or combined with desire or passion." This definition, or course, is a worldly one, and carries within it the thoughts of our contemporary society. Someone said, "If you want to see the depravity of man, look in the dictionary." Words associated with man become depraved by that association. Freud defined love as sexual love, or almost entirely sexual love.

Most human definitions of love only faintly reflect — or do not reflect at all — the meaning of love as found in the New Testament. It is quite impossible to understand the meaning of love — that is, true love — unless we are prepared to look at it in relation to Jesus Christ. John put content into the word 'love' when he quoted Christ saying: "Love one another, just as I have loved you." It is quite clear from these words that if we really want to understand what God and the Scriptures mean when they use the word 'love', then we must see it demonstrated and exemplified in the attitudes and actions of our Lord Jesus Christ.

It's interesting that while many of the world's great

John
15:1–7
v. 12

thinkers are prepared to accept that love is the highest principle in the universe, they are not prepared to link that principle to the person of Christ. They are willing to accept the principle but unwilling to accept the Person. Erich Fromm, for example, in his book *The Art of Loving*, says: "Having spoken of the love of God, I want to make it clear that I myself do not think in terms of a theistic concept, and that to me the concept of God is only a historically conditioned one, in which man has expressed his experience of his higher powers, his longing for truth and for unity at a given historical period."

1 John
1:1–10
v. 1

Can you see what he is saying? Man puts his own content into the word 'God' and is the mediator of God to himself. God, then, is all that a man sees in himself at his greatest and best moments. Those who are

unwilling to take their content of the word 'love' from Jesus Christ must get it from somewhere else. But from where? Hollywood? Television? Art? Soap operas? God forbid! The issue, it seems to me, is quite clear — we either get the content of the word 'love' from the Son of Man, or we have to get it from the sons of men. And what a sorry lot mankind has turned out to be! To take the principle of love and separate it from the Person who best exemplified it is to take a degenerated principle. Perhaps this is the new crucifixion of Jesus — to take His principles but reject His Person.

Jesus alone can reveal to us what love is, and what it is all about. Love cannot be understood or defined outside of Jesus Christ, and those who want to take the principle of love, but reject the Person who best exemplified the principle, accept a principle that is degenerate.

1 Timothy
3:1–16
v. 16

All persons, words, concepts and principles in this world have to be constantly brought to the feet of Jesus Christ so that they can be reclaimed and regenerated by Him. Things, even *good* things, go wrong when Jesus is not at the controls. One writer put it like this: "As literature can never rise higher than life, so words and principles can never rise higher than the life that surrounds the literature. Persons, words, concepts and principles sink to the level of the surrounding life and get their content from the surrounding life, unless renewed by contact with and surrender to the higher life." As Ernest Renan says: "Humanity seeks the Ideal, but it will find it, not in an abstraction, but in a Person."

The word 'love' in the English language has a medley of meanings, ranging from lust on the one hand to self-sacrifice on the other. It is used in modern parlance to describe acts of fornication, adultery, and homosexual practice, so the word needs to be redeemed. Jesus has done precisely that by taking the word 'love' and putting the content of His own love into it. Look at Him, listen to Him, live with Him, learn from Him, and you will know what love is.

One of the things that intrigues me, whenever I find myself in a pre-marital counselling situation, is the answer I get from couples when I ask them how they would define the word 'love'. They say, "Love is making your partner do what is right." "Love is giving in, rather than having a row." Norman Wright, an American marriage guidance counsellor, reports that once, when he asked a couple to define love, he got this answer: "Love is a feeling you get when you get a feeling you never felt before." A missionary told me that she was unable to use the Japanese word for love

before non-Christian audiences, because it had a strong connotation of sexual love. The word had not been in contact with Jesus and was unredeemed.

Apart from Jesus Christ, the word is inevitably devalued. Not even modern psychology can come up with a satisfying and complete definition of love, for, as Victor Krankl, a well-known psychiatrist, says: "Psychology is the favourite recourse of those with a tendency toward devaluation." He goes on also to say: "Let's apply psychology to itself by examining its own psychogenesis — that is, the motives that underlie it. What is its hidden basic attitude, its secret tendency? *A tendency toward devaluation*" (italics mine). What a condemning statement — and by someone who ranks as one of the foremost psychiatrists of our day.

Mark 7:14–23

v. 21

LOVE — *AGAPE*

It is obvious that we must turn to Christ to find the true content of the word 'love', and that is why I come back again to the words of Jesus: "Love one another, just as I have loved you."

The nearest word that we can find to describe the kind of love which Jesus exemplified when He was here on earth is the Greek word, *agape*. The word was in use during the days of Jesus, but it had a much lesser meaning then than it has now. The reason is this: that following Jesus' life, death and resurrection, Christians used the word *agape* to embody a distinctly Christian concept. With its new Christian connotation, the word stands for the most revolutionary idea ever presented to the mind of man — the idea that love is spontaneous, unmotivated and unconditional — a love that knows no boundaries, no restrictions, no barriers. As Anders Nygren put it: "The Christian idea of love . . . involves a revolution in ethical outlook without parallel in the history of ethics . . . a transvaluation of all ancient values."

John 17:15–26

Can you now see more clearly the thought we have been pursuing — that the highest ideas of men must be brought in contact with Christ before they can take on their true and fullest meaning? I believe with all my heart that one of the greatest needs in the Church today is to rediscover what the early Christians understood by that word, *agape*. To rediscover *agape* as the early Christians used the word is to uncover the answer to all effective living. Our world is sick, literally and metaphorically sick — for love. With it, we can go confidently into the future; without it — we perish.

1 Thessalonians 3:1–13
v. 12

We can lay down a Christian definition of 'love' when we lay the two Greek words *eros* and *agape* alongside each other.

Eros is acquisitive love — it longs to get; *agape* is sacrificial love — it longs to give. *Eros* is egocentric love, a form of self-assertion; *agape* is unselfish love, and seeks nothing for itself. *Eros* seeks to gain its life; *agape* lives the life of God, and therefore dares to lose it. *Eros* is the will to get and possess; *agape* is the will to distribute and dispense. *Eros* is determined by the quality, beauty and worth of its object; *agape* is sovereign in relation to its object, and is directed to both "the good and the evil". *Eros recognises* value in its object and loves it; *agape* loves and *creates* value in its object by the act of loving.

Do you see how clearly true love emerges from these comparisons? Here the issues are drawn. All systems and all life line themselves up on one side or the other. *Eros* loves for what it can get out of it. It turns everything — even God — into a means to gain its own ends. It loves people for what they can give in return; if there is no return, then love ceases. But with *agape* the case is different. God is *Agape* — He is self-giving love. When Paul said, "Love never fails", he was thinking of *agape*, not *eros*. *Eros* love does fail — and fails very often. For at the centre of *eros* are the seeds of its own failure — it is self-seeking love.

John
3:14–21
v. 16

In the light of these facts, the question you and I must ask ourselves is this: how much of my love is *eros*, and how much is *agape*? The greatest danger lies, not in our being anti-Christian, but sub-Christian.

LOVE — THE ART OF LIVING

Many know everything about life except how to live it. They fail at the vital place of life — the art of living. And what is the art of living? It is simple — the art of living is *loving*.

A group of Bible College students asked the question: how many levels are there on which people try to live? They came up with four: (1) the level of instinct; (2) the level of duty; (3) the level of faith; and (4) the level of "faith working through love". Take the first — the level of instinct. It is impossible for humanity to live effectively on this level alone. Animals can live effectively on this level: if they respond to their physical environment by taking in food and water, they will survive, and assuming there are no great dangers facing them, spend a fairly contented existence on the earth.

Man, however, being a moral and a spiritual being, is conscious of a moral as well as a physical environment — and he must respond to both if he is to live effectively on the earth. Man cannot adopt the position of an animal and say to himself: "My instincts will determine how I behave," for when he tries to act on that assumption, he finds himself in trouble. He gets tangled up in his own moral and spiritual nature and the moral universe around him. As Pascal put it: "Man is not merely a creature of instinct, but the creator of purposes." To live at the impulse of our urges is to live in perpetual trouble and frustration — yet many try it.

Psalm
8:1–9
v. 4

In a newspaper, I noticed a report about a man who took a car belonging to someone else and drove from

one end of Britain to the other because, as he put it, "I had an urge to have a drink in a pub I liked." But his 'urge' came into conflict with the law against stealing, and because he had several other convictions, he finished up in jail. Man cannot live by urges or instincts alone. He is not a self-sufficient being who can do as he likes — regardless. He cannot break the laws that have been written into the universe: he can only break himself upon them. Our inner opinions about the way the universe has been constructed do not really matter — the results or consequences register themselves in us with no regard for our opinions.

A woman shared with me recently that she had committed adultery with a married man. When I asked her how she felt about this, she replied: "Strangely, I feel no guilt at all." I said, "But you do realise you have committed adultery?" She replied, "Adultery is such an ugly word; I prefer to call it 'love'." I noticed that in spite of her euphemism, the moral facts were closing in upon her — she was agitated, nervous, defensive, and her conscience bore all the marks of being seared. On her knees before God, her defences crumbled and she took refuge, not in subterfuges, but in safety — the safety of repentance and divine forgiveness.

1 Timothy
4:1–10

v. 2

When we try to live effectively on the level of instinct, we are trying to live against the grain of the universe and it becomes a losing battle. Those who see this then try to move up to a slightly higher level — the level of duty. This is the level where we recognise that there are moral laws in the universe and do our best to obey them.

Galatians
3:1–14
v. 3

Obviously this is a higher form of living than living on the level of instinct, but the trouble is that many Christians believe this to be the level on which the Christian life should operate; needless to say, they soon come to grief. They go to church, pray, give to good causes and strive to live an upright and moral life. They are constantly whipping up their wills in an effort to be good, pushing themselves into spiritual achievement and driving their personalities toward the goal of being like Christ. But so many of them finish up depleted — physically and spiritually. Instead of Christianity relieving the strain, it becomes simply another area of conflict and tension.

Am I describing your condition at this moment? Then listen carefully to what I have to say — when we do our duty toward God without drawing our resources from Him, our religion becomes self-centred instead of God-centred. In a religion that is lived merely on the level of duty, God is marginal and we are central. Duty is a better level of living than instinct, but not the highest level. God says: "Come up higher."

We look now at the third level — the level of faith. I am thinking of faith here in terms of receptivity —

openness to all of God's power and resources. This is the level where you do not whip up your will, but surrender your will. This makes you relaxed and receptive, able to assimilate all that God has to give you.

Galatians 2:15–21
v. 21

Someone described this level of living thus: "Faith is not restless but recuperative: around your emptiness flows His fulness; around your incompleteness, His completeness; around your restlessness, His rest; around your sin, His holiness; around your self, His Self; around your lovelessness, His love." On this level of living, there is no strain — we live fully and overflowingly.

The difference between the stages of duty and faith is most clearly illustrated in the life of John Wesley, before and after his experience of conversion at Aldersgate. Before conversion, John Wesley was meticulous in trying to be good. His life, however, was a failure

because he worked under the lash of duty. Then came the moment at Aldersgate, where he saw in a way he had never understood before the meaning of Christ's death and atonement. He emptied his hands and took the gift of eternal life. Then what happened? One biographer says: "He walked out of that little meeting house, threw his leg over the back of a horse, and went out to save England." He was lifted from the level of duty to the level of faith; no longer restless, but receptive.

The goodness that flows from our lives when once we are linked to Christ by faith is not artificial, but artesian — it bubbles up from within because it *must*. Work and witness spring from infinite resources within us — the more we give, the more we have to give.

So many of us are exhausted by our problems, but fail

John 1:9–17

v. 16

to see that really the exhaustion comes from within, not without. All our problems on the outside can be handled if the problems on the inside have been resolved. Remember the old story of the Trojan horse? The wooden horse in which the enemies lay concealed was drawn into the city by the unsuspecting Trojans, and during the dead of night, the enemies came out and captured the city. How many Christians are defeated day after day, not by their outside circumstances, but by their inner circumstances? They carry conflicts on the inside, and thus they are unable to deal with the conflicts on the outside.

Speaking of Christian action, Pascal said: "All men of action are men of receptivity." Can you see what he meant? All their action has upon it the mark of self-surrender, and not self-advancement. Hence people look beyond them to the grace and power of God that is working through them.

It would appear then that the level of faith is the highest level on which to live — but not so. I have come to see that there is a higher level even than that — the level of "faith working through love". This is the highest level.

Galatians
5:1–13
v. 6

I used to hold that faith was the method by which Christianity advanced in the world, and that all Christians must strive to get faith. In those days I had a strong and vigorous faith, but I regret to say that it did not "work through love". My faith was aggressive, combative and pushy, and although it accomplished things, others got hurt in the process.

Then the Lord took me aside and showed me "a more excellent way". He said: "The faith that you have is fine, but it lacks love. Listen to my word . . . 'These three remain: faith, hope and love. But the greatest of these is

love.'" I listened to what the Lord had to say, meditated upon it and came to see that love is the applied edge of faith. As D.L. Moody put it: "Love is faith in shoes — going out to serve the least, the last and the lost." If everything that does not have love in it is a sounding gong and a tinkling cymbal, then what good is faith without love?

Many Christians have a working faith that does not work through love. It works by combat, by aggressiveness against those who do not see eye to eye with them about their faith. The Christian faith does not need protection; it needs proclamation. It is its own defence. You don't have to protect a lion from other animals in the jungle — it is well able to take care of itself. The Church is filled with nervous

Christians who, like Uzziah, stretch out their hands to steady the ark.

2 Samuel 6:6

I am quite convinced myself that if Christians made sure they were operating, not just on the level of faith, but on the level of "faith working through love", then modern-day evangelism would be a hundred times more effective. A minister of a large evangelical church tells how one day a man said to him: "I feel you are out for my spiritual scalp — but I don't feel that you really love me as a person." He reported this conversation to his church elders, who immediately felt convicted and fell on their knees in repentance. When they later reported it to the whole church, it caused them to enter upon a week of prayer and fasting. The result? A mighty baptism of love.

Romans 5:1–11
v. 5

LOVE — HOW?

Our meditation on this divine, *agape* love is best put in
the form of a question. If love is such an important
quality, then how do we go about the task of loving? It's
easy to command, but how do we live up to that
command? Can we just switch on love as we do an
electric light?

Quite honestly, when I read or heard the greatest
commandment preached on in my youth, a nagging
question arose within me: how can you command love?
You can command a person to do this and that, or not to
do this and not to do that — but can you really *command*
a person to love?

John tells us in his first letter, written to new
Christians, that "his commands are not burdensome".
On the surface of it, this statement seems somewhat
contradictory. The command to love God with all our
heart, all our mind, all our soul, all our strength and to
love our neighbour as ourselves seems, at first sight, to
be the heaviest command ever laid upon the human
heart. And yet John quietly and decisively says: "his
commands are not burdensome."

1 John
5:1–12
v. 3

What, then, is the answer to this seeming
contradiction? Is it not this — that the God who asks us
to love also provides the power to do what He
commands? I do not have to love — I have to allow love
to love me into loving. In other words, the command to
love does not mean that we have to reach deep down
within ourselves to create feelings of love for God, but
rather we should focus on how much He loves us and let
His love love us into loving.

John Powell, in his book *Why Am I Afraid to Love?*

says: "Before anyone can really give his heart, soul and mind to the task of loving God, he must first know how much God has loved him, how God has thought about him from all eternity and desired to share His life, joy and love with him." It is precisely at this point that so many Christians go astray. Whenever a person says to me: "My problem is that I do not love the Lord enough", I usually respond: "No, that's not your problem — your problem is that you don't know how much the Lord loves you."

Christians who are not aware of God's fatherly, even *tender* love — who conceive of Him as a fearsome and frowning figure — will almost invariably have difficulty in feeling and expressing love toward God, and, for that matter, toward others also. Pascal, the great Christian philosopher, made the point somewhere in his writings that there is no human being who will not eventually respond to love if only he can realise that he is loved. Instead of constantly reminding youself: "I must love", focus on telling yourself: "I am loved." Then note the difference.

1 John
4:10–19
v. 19

LOVE — THE DIFFICULTY

Why is it that so many Christians find difficulty in receiving and giving love? There can be many answers to this perplexing issue, but in my experience the *main* reason why Christians get into difficulty here is due to the fact that their early lives were marked by an absence of human love, with all of its life-giving effects.

Psalm 27:1–14 v. 10

I am not saying that our early environment determines us in a way that cannot be altered, for I believe with Scripture that what was caused can be changed. I have noticed, however, when counselling Christians who have difficulty in receiving and giving love, that almost invariably they have a history of deprivation in the area of human love.

Each of us carries within ourselves our own unique and very limited concept of God, and this concept is often influenced and distorted by negative experiences in our developmental years. Those who do not take the steps to see God in the way He is presented in Scripture will limp along in the shadow of a frowning Providence and will find it difficult to love with their whole heart, soul and mind. They have never experienced the deep sense of *belonging* to a Father who is entirely trustworthy, entirely loving and *who is always there*.

Those who have never experienced human love must not, of course, make what has happened in the past an excuse for not opening up in the present, as through Christ's death on the Cross, God has given us all the evidence we need to know that we are loved. Although you may have experienced the pain of not being loved in the past, you need never experience it again, for if you

John 14:1–14 v. 9

are a Christian then you have Him — who is love!

Having said this, however, I am not insensitive to the fact that there are many who, because of past failures in love, find it a great struggle to develop the concept of a God who loves. Scripture tells us that God made us in His image and likeness, but human nature tends to invert this, and we finish up by making God in our image and likeness. We project the fears and uncertainties of our past relationships on to God, and serve Him out of fear, rather than love.

The person who serves God out of fear (i.e. neurotic fear, not godly fear) and without the realisation of love will often try to bargain with God — do little things for Him, say prayers, make sacrifices — all with a view to obtaining His approval. The Christian life becomes a chess game rather than an affair of love. If you are one of these people, then you must make a decision now to reject such an unworthy concept of God, and put your weight on Scripture rather than on your feelings or your negative experiences.

LOVE — THE CURE FOR FEAR

What is the most debilitating emotion that can arise within the human heart? I would say without hesitation — fear. But what is fear? Many answers and definitions can be given to that question, but I believe myself that fear is basically the absence of love. When love is allowed to invade our beings, fear can have no root; when fear is allowed to invade our beings, love can have no root.

1 John 4:18

What is behind fear? This — the pain of believing that one is not loved. And nothing can cure that fear except a deep-down assurance that we *are* loved. This is where the Christian Gospel comes into its own, for it gives us just the assurance we need. This assurance, by the way, is not merely a verbal one — words written down in a book — but a vital one — the Word who became flesh. God became incarnate to reveal to us His love — His agape.

Now we know that God loves us — loves us not because we are good and worthy, but because He cannot help but love. That cures our central pain — the pain of not being loved. "We are loved by Him", says one commentator, "not because we are good, not when we are deserving, not if we do this, that and the other, not because of anything we are, do or say, but simply because He *is* love. He cannot do anything other than love us and be God." When we get hold of this assurance and it gets hold of us, the fear of not being loved is cancelled out in our personalities, for we are loved no matter what we do or become. But it does something else, something marvellous and exciting — His love produces love in us in return.

However, it is not our love for Him that casts out fear,

but His love for us. It is *perfect* love that drives out fear. Love — His love — begets love. This, then, is the answer to the question why we love — *because* He first loved us.

1 John 4:19

The statement "perfect love casts out fear" is an intriguing one, because the words present a departure from what we would naturally expect. When it begins, "There is no fear in . . ." we would expect it to go on to say, "There is no fear in faith." We usually try to match faith against fear — why, then, does this verse speak about love? Our fear, basically, is the fear of not being loved — and only love can cure that. I allow His love to flow in, and inevitably the fear of not being loved flows out.

There is still more: the moment I open my being to focus on how much God loves me, I begin in some strange way to love with His love. I love God with the love of God, and I also love others with the love of God. A missionary tells how, on her arrival in China many years ago, she was taken in a rickshaw through the crowded streets of the city, and as she viewed the people a wave of revulsion swept over her. "O God", she cried, "how can I love these people — they are so revolting. I can't even begin to love them unless You help me." As she sat in the rickshaw, a fresh sense of how much God loved her invaded her being. She was instantly changed — and for the rest of her days, she loved them with God's love.

As he surveyed the wonder of Christ's death, the great apostle John burst out in a doxology of praise: "This Man loved me!" Fear is banished in the awareness of such love. Perfect love — *His* love — casts out fear.

LOVE — WROTE PAUL

The thirteenth chapter of First Corinthians is one of the greatest expositions of love in the whole of literature — sacred and secular. When Dr E. Stanley Jones, the famous missionary to India, read this chapter to Mahatma Gandhi, the great leader showed evidence of deep emotion, and with tears in his eyes said: "How beautiful; how beautiful."

We cannot fully understand the opening words of 1 Corinthians 13 until we know something of the age in which Paul was writing. There were three dominant races at the time — the Greeks, the Jews and the Romans. The Greeks emphasised the power of speech and oratory; the Jews emphasised the power of the prophetic word; and the Romans emphasised the way of military might and action, being willing to sacrifice their own lives for the sake of the nation's honour.

1 Corinthians 13

Paul stepped into the midst of these three emphases and said: "If I speak in the tongues of men (the Greeks) and of angels, but have not love, I am only a resounding gong . . . If I have the gift of prophecy (the Jews) and can fathom all mysteries and all knowledge, and if I have a faith that can move mountains, but have not love, I am nothing. If I give all I possess to the poor and surrender my body to the flames (the Romans), but have not love, I gain nothing".

vv. 1–3

In these dramatic words of Paul, the ancient world was weighed and found wanting. A more devastating judgment was never given, for against the new and more excellent way which Jesus Christ had opened up — the way of love — the lesser ways led nowhere. Paul showed in these glowing words that the future lies with love. For only love remains.

There was also tension in the spiritual background against which Paul was writing — the divided church of Corinth. It must have been extremely painful for the apostle to hear of the waywardness and sinful practices of some of the Corinthian Christians. Some of the things the Christians were getting involved in were deeply disappointing and disturbing, to say the least. Out of Paul's pain, however, comes a chapter that is regarded by many as the greatest treatise on love ever written. One commentator says of it: "You simply cannot write such literature as this — except out of a heart of pain."

2 Corinthians 7:1–12

v. 10

In 1 Corinthians 13, Paul spells out sixteen things about love — eight things it does do, and eight things it does not do. Love always seeks to be positive, but there are times when it has to be negative. To put no negatives in love makes love sentimental. A father said to his wayward son, "We love you, but we don't like what you have done today." That is love — sensible, not sentimental. "The negatives in love", said someone, "are the hedges along the path so that love will not stray."

LOVE IS . . .

The first thing Paul says about love is that it is *patient*. Why is love patient? Because love which has a Christian content knows that in spite of the present, the future belongs to Christ. It knows that nothing wrong can come out right, and nothing right can come out wrong.

Love is also *kind*. The act of patience is one thing; the attitude is another. Being 'kind' in the act of patience is what produces the aroma which gives it sweetness. Have you met patient people who left you unimpressed? They are patient types, but there is no 'kindness' in the patience — therefore it is something less than love.

The next statement of Paul's is a negative one: "Love is not jealous, boastful or proud."* Both jealousy and boastfulness show one thing — a sense of inferiority. If you are jealous of someone, you probably feel inferior to them. Boastfulness is the other side of the coin — you boast to cover up your feelings of inferiority. Pride prevents you from seeing yourself as you really are, and thus militates against true humility. The next point made by the great apostle is this: "Love is not arrogant or rude." Arrogance is something inward and need not be expressed in words. Boastfulness needs words, but arrogance does not. Arrogance is an attitude that expresses itself in rude and insulting actions. The arrogant and rude are unsure of themselves. Only the humble are sure of themselves, and only those who are sure of themselves are humble.

At the centre of these statements is another beautiful phrase: "Love does not demand its own way." The victory

1 Corinthians 13:4

v. 5

v. 5

*The phrases followed in this exposition of 1 Corinthians 13 are from a number of translations.

of love is the victory over an insistent demand to have one's own way. The best way to get your own way is to surrender the desire into the hands of Christ. Then you will want not your way, but His way.

So we come to another characteristic of love: "Love is not irritable or resentful." The core of all resentment and irritation is an unsurrendered self. This is why it is pointless to fight resentment and irritation; instead, surrender the touchy, insecure self into Christ's hands, and the irritability and resentments will drop away. Surrender the root, and the fruit will drop away — it is no longer being fed.

Another thing love does not do is this: "Love does not rejoice at wrong, but rejoices in the right." Some Christians fall into the attitude of always looking for wrong and are disappointed when they cannot find it —

v. 5

v. 6

especially in other Christians. What is the unconscious motive behind this? It is this: if I can find something wrong in others, then this proves my spiritual superiority; their wrongness boosts my rightness. The test of whether we are acting through love or through a desire to boost ourselves is simple: in pointing out wrong in others, do I become a more loving person? If not, then love is not the basis of my attitudes and actions. Love rejoices in the right and, by its attitudes, produces the thing it rejoices in.

Next Paul turns to focus on four positive things about love — "Love bears all things, believes all things, hopes all things, endures all things." Why can love bear all things? Because it knows that it can *use* all things. Love is so powerful that it can take everything and turn it to advantage. It does with evil what Jesus did with it — turns it into good. It makes every Good Friday into an Easter Sunday.

The first and last words of this statement are similar: "bears . . . endures". The two central words are also similar: "believes . . . hopes".

1 Corinthians 13:7

The reason why love bears and endures all things is because it has a belief and a hope that all things are being worked out according to God's purposes. This saves the bearing and enduring of life's problems from being stoical, and makes it Christian. A stoic just endures things; the Christian endures — but, at the same time, exults.

Someone once defined democracy as "that madness which believes about people that which is not true, and yet without that belief, they will never become what we believe them to be". If this is true of democracy, then how much truer is it of love. Love sees an Augustine in every libertine, and a saint in every sinner. It has a deathless hope at its heart. In fact, as someone has pointed out, the only faith that uses hope as a working force is the Christian faith. In Romans 8:3, Paul reminds us that "in hope we were saved". In another chapter of Romans, Paul prays: "May the God of hope fill you with all joy and peace in believing, so that by the power of the Holy Spirit you may abound in hope" (Rom. 15:13). Love believes and hopes because it knows that God has the last word in everything.

Romans 8:18–39

v. 24

Romans 15:13

"Love never fails." I remember many years ago preaching a sermon on this text to a group of young people, and afterwards, during the discussion time, the question was raised as to whether this claim of Paul's was true. The questioner said: "I have tried to show love to a boy at my school who ridicules me, scoffs at me, swears at me — but the more love I show, the worse he becomes. In my

1 Corinthians 13:8

case, the love I show seems to fail."

I pointed out to him that the text did not say that love guarantees to bring about in people all the changes we would like to see, for God has made men and women with free wills, which means they are free to either receive or reject the power of love. What I believe this text means by saying that "love never fails" is that the more we love, the more loving we become, so that even if we receive no responses to our love, we have not loved in vain — we are the more loving for having loved.

A cultured and refined woman said to a preacher who had also been preaching on this text: "Your sermon this morning touched my heart. I am going home to love my husband with a deeper love than I have ever given him before. If he responds — good, but if he doesn't respond, it will still be good, for I'll be the better for giving it." It sounds, on the surface, as if she was attempting to use love to serve her own ends — to gain maturity. But not really. She had simply seen the truth about love: that in loving, one can never lose. As Mary Reed, missionary to the lepers of the Himalayas, once put it: "Christians are such incorrigible lovers."

Ephesians 2:1–10
vv. 4–5

Paul says that prophecy will pass away, tongues will cease and knowledge will also pass away. What a death-blow these words give to many of our modern quests! To be told that our scientific achievements, our insights into the world's workings, our predictions of the future, our great conquests of time and space will all pass away, is to pull the rug out from under humanity's feet with a vengeance.

1 Corinthians 13:8

1 John 2:7–17
v. 17

Picture a nuclear scientist presenting his knowledge of how to split the atom before God and saying: "Here,

Lord, this is what I did for You when I was down there on the earth." What do you think the Lord would say in reply? Perhaps this: "Tell me, how much love was there behind your knowledge?"

I suspect that if this kind of situation were to take place, multitudes of the scientific fraternity would stand condemned. And not just scientists, but a whole host of other professions too — schoolteachers, bankers, politicians, businessmen and so on. Of what use is our knowledge unless there is love behind it to control and direct it to the good of humanity? Yes, knowledge will pass away, and only faith, hope and love will remain. The greatest of these is *love*.

LOVE — IN EPHESUS

We move on now to focus on one of the greatest
churches of the New Testament — the church at
Ephesus. Do you recall how this great church began? It
began with the apostle Paul laying his hands upon
twelve very spiritual but ineffective disciples, and
praying for them to receive the Holy Spirit. There are
two groups of twelve spoken of in the book of Acts: the
twelve apostles who were busy 'turning the world upside
down', and the twelve disciples at Ephesus, who were
turning nothing upside down. Why the difference? The
answer is simple: one group had been filled with the
Spirit — the other hadn't.

After Paul prayed for the believers at Ephesus, the
Holy Spirit came upon them and set their lives on fire.
As a result, a spiritual awakening took place that spread
through the whole city — so much so that many people
who practised magical arts came and publicly burned
books worth a total of fifty thousand pieces of silver. We
read: "In this way the word of the Lord spread widely and
grew in power" (Acts 19:20). What a beginning!

Acts 19:20

Some years later, however, we see a different picture.
In Revelation 2:1–7, the Lord Jesus charges the
Ephesians, through John, with being a 'fallen' church —
fallen in the thing that matters most — love. No matter
how busy and spiritually industrious a church may be,
when it falls away from love it misses the central point of
the faith. Without love, all our services and activities are
a sounding gong and a tinkling cymbal.

Revelation 2:1–7

"Yet I hold this against you: You have forsaken your
first love." The words of the risen Lord to the Ephesian

church were strong and deeply challenging: "Remember the height from which you have fallen! Repent and do the things you did at first. If you do not repent, I will come to you and remove your lampstand from its place" (Rev. 2:4 & 5).

Revelation 2:4 & 5

There were, of course, many positive things that the Lord had to say about the Ephesian Christians — they were hard-working, patient and enduring, they would not put up with evildoers, and they were intolerant of sin. By some standards, the Ephesian church would have been regarded as a progressive and deeply spiritual group of people, but as far as Jesus was concerned, it was a 'fallen' church.

Ephesians 5:1–14
v. 2

If we were to apply that same standard to our churches today, I wonder how many of them our Lord would label as 'fallen'? Half of them? Three-quarters? How do you think your own church would fare in a test such as this? A church can be orthodox in doctrine, efficient in service, blameless in character, beautiful in ritual, rich in culture, eloquent in preaching — yet all these things are but the ashes on a rusty altar if it knows nothing of a burning, blazing love for the Lord Jesus Christ.

How did Jesus deal with the Ephesian church? He commanded them to 'repent' — repent of their lovelessness. He goes on to say that if they do not repent, He will come and "remove your lampstand from its place". What was that lampstand? *It was the church itself*: "The seven lampstands are the seven churches" Rev. 1:20). And how does our Lord remove the churches? By withdrawing from them His divine presence. Thus — as He said to another church: "You have a reputation of being alive, but you are dead" (Rev. 3:1).

Revelation 1:20

Revelation 3:1

Jesus ends His challenge with an offer: "To him who overcomes, I will give the right to eat from the tree of life, which is in the paradise of God" (Rev. 2:7). When the church at Ephesus abandoned the love it first had for the Lord Jesus Christ, it abandoned its very life; it shut itself off from the tree of life. Instead it fed itself on the husks of orthodoxy, efficiency and activity — poor substitutes for the life which flows through love. They hated the things which Christ hated, but failed to love the things which Christ loved. Indeed, their biggest failure was their lack of love toward the Lord Himself.

1 Timothy 1:3–4 help us to understand why the Ephesian Christians had gone off the track. Paul urges Timothy to remain at Ephesus and try to get the members into the way of loving once again. These words concerning the

Revelation 2:7

1 Timothy 1:1–11 vv. 3 & 4

Ephesian Christians, remember, were written years prior to the words of our Lord in the book of Revelation.

Listen to Paul's words once again, this time in an early edition of the Moffatt translation: "Warn certain individuals against teaching novelties and studying myths . . . such studies bear upon speculations rather than on the divine training which belongs to faith. Whereas the aim of the Christian discipline is the love that springs from a pure heart, from a good conscience, and from a sincere faith" (vv. 3–5). Paul says that the 'divine training' is a training in love — "a love that springs . . ." — which issues out to every person, everywhere.

vv. 3–5

I have no doubt that Timothy would have passed on Paul's words to the Ephesians — but did they heed them? It seems not. They missed the way, and thus soon fell away.

That a lack of response to the 'divine training' was the possible reason for the lovelessness among the Ephesian believers is extremely important, for it shows us that the whole aim of the Christian discipline is to produce people who love.

We must ask ourselves: how does this 'divine training' take place? Does it mean that God lays down certain laws and principles that we must follow? Yes, that is part of the training, but not the primary part. The 'divine training' is not only a training in love, but a training by love. We have seen that when we respond to His love for us, our love for Him grows. We do things — or we do not do things — because we love Him. It is not so much the applying of this law or that law, this restraint or that restraint, it is a 'divine training' from within flowing outwards, not from without flowing inwards.

One who is trained by opening his heart to Christ's love cries out: "The love of Christ controls me." Such a person is trained in a natural and spontaneous way — not compelled to love, but impelled to love. Oh, why do so many Christians miss this truth? We gaze at how much He loves us, and the scales fall from our eyes: our own love flames in response. Christians trained in this way find that loving is the easiest thing they do — and the most profound. They love, as Jesus loves, *because* . . . they cannot help but love.

2 Corinthians
5:11–21
v. 14

LOVE — SPRINGS

When we allow Christ to love us as only He can love, then love 'springs' from a pure heart, a good conscience and a sincere faith. You don't have to force yourself to love: it is a love that *springs*.

Matthew 11:25–30

Some people might find the words 'discipline' and 'springs' in this passage to be at variance with one another. 'Discipline' speaks of law, while 'springs' speaks of freedom. Let's take the word 'discipline' first. Someone said: "The future of the world is in the hands of disciplined people. The undisciplined waste their energies with themselves and their own tangles." The first part of that statement needs to be corrected: "The future of the world is in the hands of disciplined people — *those who are disciplined to the Highest*."

If one is not disciplined by the Highest — Jesus Christ — then the discipline will exhaust itself. To what end is the Christian disciplined? Listen to the words again, this time in a later edition of the Moffatt translation — "the divine order which belongs to faith" (1 Tim. 1:4). And what is the divine order which belongs to faith? The principles of Scripture as embodied and exemplified in the person of Jesus Christ. Don't forget that, for the divine order cannot be separated from the divine Person — Jesus. We are therefore disciplined by a Person who embodies a divine order — an embodiment which makes our discipline personal. We are disciplined by the One who loves us as no one else loves us.

1 Timothy 1:4

That makes discipline, not just a duty, but a delight. It is total and complete as it reaches in to control the deepest thoughts.

Does this mean that it produces robots — puppets

dancing on the invisible strings of the divine Master backstage? No! Look again at how Paul expresses the spontaneity of the Christian discipline: "the love that *springs*". It produces spontaneity — it *springs*.

 John 7:37–49

St Augustine put it like this: "Love God and do as you like." This is perfect freedom — we are free to do what we ought. How sad that the Ephesian church failed to heed the message that Paul and Timothy brought to it. If they had given themselves to the Christian discipline, then they would not have abandoned their love, they would have advanced in it. When we surrender our whole being to Jesus Christ and allow Him to love in us and through us, we become the most spontaneous and natural people in the universe. The law ends in liberty — a "love that springs". We love because we cannot help it.

LOVE — THE WORD

When we were seeking to define the nature of love, we described some of the differences between the two words *eros* and *agape*. E.S. Jones makes this interesting comment on these two words: "The difference between *eros* and *agape* can never be truly understood by words — it has to be seen. Agape had to become flesh. Then, and then only, could it be known what Agape really is." How true. If Christ had not become flesh, then *agape* would have been just an interesting concept — a sweet dream. In the incarnation of Christ, however, the dream becomes a deed.

John 8:31 is an important verse. Listen to it in the New English Bible translation: "If you dwell within the revelation I have brought, you are indeed my disciples; you shall know the truth and the truth will set you free." Note the words: "If you dwell within the revelation *I have brought*". What was the 'revelation' He had brought? Was it like the revelations other spiritual leaders had brought — such as Moses, Elijah and Isaiah? No, for they brought simply a word — Jesus was the Word become flesh. That sets this 'revelation' apart and makes it unique. You can't put Jesus alongside other great spiritual leaders, for they are not in the same category. They taught — Jesus brought. And the words He spoke were part of the bringing — for His words were the revelation of His own self, every word operative within Himself.

John 8:28–36
v. 31

In India many years ago, a missionary spoke at a meeting which was chaired by a Hindu Member of State. The chairman said afterwards: "I could not help but contrast this meeting tonight with the meetings I

attended as a boy. Then we used to heckle the missionaries and throw rotten fruit at them. But here this great audience sits in pin-drop silence, listening to the Christian message. What has made the difference? Perhaps it is this: nearby is the great Miraj mission hospital where Christian doctors attend to poor and rich, night and day. Not so long ago, when I was going through a small town, I saw a lady missionary coming out of a house with her hands extended. She came up to me and said: 'I'm sorry I can't shake hands with you, for my hands are plague-stained.' When I saw those plague-stained hands, I saw the meaning of the Christian faith."

Through the particular he saw the Universal. It is the

only possible way it can be seen. In Jesus Christ — the Word made flesh — the Universal is made clear in the particular. His loving acts portray the highest meaning of life.

John 6:35–47

v. 46

Students of American history will remember that at Gettysburg, two men spoke — Abraham Lincoln and Edward Hale. Abraham Lincoln, in his Gettysburg address, used very few words, but they are words that have lived on and will never be forgotten. Although Edward Hale, according to his biographer, was a more eloquent speaker than Lincoln, few can remember what he said that day. The reason? In Edward Hale, men heard about freedom and democracy; in Lincoln, they did not just hear it — they saw it.

If a man in love with his wife and away from home were offered a book on the subject of married love, would he not say something like this: "I appreciate your offer, but what I long for more than words or pictures is my wife."

Years ago, when I was a pastor in central London, the young people of the church started an outreach among the drug addicts of Soho. Almost every night, they would go down into the rented basement of an old church, and minister to these addicts, giving them free coffee and sandwiches and sharing with them the good news of Jesus Christ. At first the addicts viewed them with suspicion, calling them 'do-gooders'. I heard one addict say, "They can't be for real." But when they saw these young people come night after night to where they were, and though dead tired and weary, stay with them until the early hours, one of them spoke up for the rest when he said: "Now I see the meaning of Christianity." When a word becomes flesh, it burns through the most resistant of materials, just as when a magnifying glass gathers up the sun's scattered rays and focuses them upon a single point.

Luke 1:67–79
v. 68

If *agape* love is the highest value in the universe, how could God have got us to understand that truth if He had not come to us and spelt it out in the person of His Son? Words get meaning from the life that surrounds them. A Sunday school teacher tells of how she asked a group of children who lived in a poor part of London whether they would like to go to heaven. When one of them enquired, "What's heaven like?" she replied, "It's like a home — only it's God's home." The little child said, "Then I don't want to go." To him, the word 'home' meant 'hell'; it took its meaning from the life that surrounded it.

Suppose God had just given us the Old Testament with its beautiful descriptions of love — would that have sufficed? Hardly, for we read into words our highest experience of those words. We would see the word 'love', and we would read into it our highest experience of love. But our highest experience of love is not love — at least, not love in the sense that God is love; our highest experience of love is only partial and incomplete. We tend to interpret all words according to the level of our experience.

What, then, do we need for a perfect revelation of love? We need a life to come among us — a divine life that will lift the word from the level to which we have dragged it, and put a new content into it — a divine content through a divine illustration.

Galatians
3:23—4:7
4:4

LOVE — DIVINE

Without doubt one of the most glorious verses in the John 1:1–18 whole of the New Testament is John 1:18: "No one has v. 18 ever seen God; but God's only Son, he who is nearest to the Father's heart, he has made him known (NEB)."

The Bible is a verbal revelation of God — the Word become words — but Christ is a vital revelation of God — the Word become flesh. One great theologian said in a Christmas Day sermon: "You see, you cannot describe God, you can only show Him, make Him known. And Jesus is God made known in the best way He can be known — by Life."

What do you really want to know about God? His omnipotence? It would scare you to death if you really knew how much God could do. His omniscience? Your mind would not be able to contain His knowledge, not even a billionth part of it. His omnipresence? How could you, limited as you are to a human body, understand the fact that He is everywhere at once? These three things would leave you prostrate. Isn't it true that what you *really* want to know about God is what His character is like? Jesus 'makes known' the character of God, and makes it known in the only way character can be known — namely, through another character — His own. And the essence of that character? Unconditional love.

What a beautiful phrase Moffatt uses to describe the John 1:18 relationship of Christ to God: ". . . the only Son, who lies upon the Father's breast." The term 'breast' represents the heart of God. Jesus did not come primarily to reveal the might of the Father's arm. That was part of His purpose, but not the primary one. Jesus did not come either to reveal the Father's mind. That, too, was part of His purpose — but again, not the primary one. Jesus came primarily to reveal the Father's heart — to 'make known' to us that the heartbeat of our Creator is a heartbeat of love.

When Jesus came into the world, he stripped Himself of everything — omnipotence (all-power), omniscience (all-knowledge), omnipresence (all-presence) — everything, that is, except love. As Charles Wesley put it in his beautiful hymn: "Emptied Himself . . . of all but love" — His only protection, His only weapon, His only method.

LOVE — MATURING

Maturity in life — particularly the Christian life — means maturity in love. We are mature to the extent that we can love. Sometimes, however, we love with the wrong kind of love — a love that is self-seeking and therefore immature. As a marriage guidance counsellor for many years, I have been driven to the conclusion that many marriages go on the rocks because one or both of the partners have not grown up — except physically. Immaturity, in fact, is high on the list of causes of marriage breakdown — immaturity in relationships, immaturity in understanding, immaturity in love.

Ephesians 4:14–24
v. 15

Immaturity in love is made evident in a number of ways. Firstly, it shows itself in being preponderantly physical. When love is weighted toward the physical — eros love — and is not held in control by spiritual love — agape — it is a fitful, immature kind of love and soon fizzles out. "Physical love is all you think of", said a disappointed wife to her husband as she tried to warn him that their marriage was heading for disaster. So it is not enough just to love — we must love with the right kind of love — agape love.

Another mark of immaturity is a demanding attitude. This kind of love is weighted toward the attitude of wanting to be loved. It is a possessive love: "I want him — or her — for myself." The emphasis here, consciously or unconsciously, is on what I can get out of it. Mature love is weighted towards self-forgetfulness and self-sacrifice.

The other day I read the story of Harold Groves, a missionary to India, who travelled from Calcutta to Bombay to visit some friends. The hosts sent their servant to the railway station to meet him, and when he

asked how he might recognise the missionary, they said: "Look for a white man helping somebody — that will be him." The servant saw a white man helping an old lady step down from the train, went up to him and said: "Are you Mr Groves?" — and he was.

If you want to recognise a mature person — one who is mature in love — look for someone who is helping someone else. We are as mature as we are mature in sacrificial love. The German author, Fritz Kungel, says: "The abnormality of the child's environment may be described generally as the absence of the right kind of love." The abnormality in any environment — home, business, church — is the absence of the right kind of love — mature love. When we are mature in love, we are mature indeed.

Colossians 3:1–17
v. 14

Our attitudes to life are mature or immature according to the degree of sacrificial love that is present.

1 Corinthians
11:23–34

It is important to see, however, that what we may regard consciously as self-sacrifice may really be a device to draw attention to ourselves. I have known many Christians in my time who engaged in sacrificial service, but at the same time held an attitude of pride in the very sacrifice they were making. That is not really self-sacrifice; it is self-aggrandisement. We push ourselves forward by pretending to hold ourselves back.

Self-sacrifice is also forgetfulness of self. Years ago, I knew a Christian businessman who looked around for the biggest church in the area which offered the greatest opportunity for the sale of his goods among the members. He wanted to use the church as a basis for building up his business. His attitude was not, what can I give, but, what can I get? And that attitude, I have no hesitation in saying, is as far removed from mature love as chalk is from cheese.

LOVE — GOD

It is possible also to have an immature love even while
engaged in Christian work. I have met and talked to
many Christians who have confessed that they have
more love for the work of God than they have for God
Himself.

It is possible to love Christian work for the wrong
reason. We may love it for what we get out of it —
self-display, approval or the admiration of others. This
may be a strong challenge to those who are involved in
Christian work, but nevertheless it is one that has to be
faced. A Christian must be involved in Christian work
because he loves Christ, and even if all he gets out of it is
the privilege of showing his love for Christ, he should
still do it joyfully and without regret.

We must be careful that we do not love the Christian
cause more than we love people. A few days ago I listened
to a tape of a leading minister speaking at a large
conference of his denomination, in which he confessed:
"In the early part of my ministry I was caught up in the
thrill of the Christian cause – moving forward the
Christian Church in the world. But, to my shame I admit
it, I was more project-oriented than people-oriented.
Projects came first – people next. God met me one day
and showed me how immature was my love. I thought I
was well advanced in love, but the Lord showed me that
instead of advancing, I was retreating. If that interview
with the Almighty had not taken place, I tremble to
think where I and the church I pastor would be today." I
don't wonder that this minister is sought after by many
churches.

We end our study of *Divine Love* with a final

1 Peter 1:13–25
v. 22

challenge. To see whether our love is mature love —
agape love — read 1 Corinthians 13 once again in the
New International Version, replacing the word 'love' in
verses 4–7 with the word 'I'. Prepare yourself for a
shock: "I am patient and kind; I do not envy, I do not
boast; I am not arrogant or rude. I do not insist on my
own way; I am not irritable or resentful; I do not rejoice
at wrong, but rejoice in the right. I bear all things,
believe all things, hope all things, endure all things."

1 Corinthians
13:4–7

How do you come out? Are you and love identical? Our
growth in maturity is a growth in that very
identification. I once heard a minister ask his whole
church to recite this passage together, substituting the
word 'we' for the word 'love'. He said: "If you don't
honestly think our church can come up to this standard,
then don't say it."

The whole group started out reciting the first line
together, but as they went on, scores of people dropped
out. The passage was never finished, because the
minister himself, after reciting just a few phrases, broke
down and wept. There was no preaching that morning;
instead, people fell upon their knees and asked God's
forgiveness for their lack of genuine, mature love. I tell
you, that meeting was the nearest I have ever been to
heaven!

The theologian, Emil Brunner, once said: "Find and
join the church that has the most love in it, and that will
be the truest church." Our destiny is clear: where love is,
there is the truest church; and where love is, there is the
truest Christian. Follow after love . . .